The Bald Eagle
An American Symbol

Alison and Stephen Eldridge

Enslow Elementary

an imprint of

Enslow Publishers, Inc.
40 Industrial Road
Box 398
Berkeley Heights, NJ 07922
USA

http://www.enslow.com

Enslow Elementary, an imprint of Enslow Publishers, Inc.
Enslow Elementary® is a registered trademark of Enslow Publishers, Inc.

Library of Congress Cataloging-in-Publication Data
Eldridge, Alison.
  The bald eagle : an American symbol / by Alison and Stephen Eldridge.
    p. cm. — (All About American symbols)
  Includes index.
  Summary: "Introduces pre-readers to simple concepts about the importance of the bald eagle using short
sentences and repetition of words"—Provided by publisher.
  ISBN 978-0-7660-4058-8
  1. United States—Seal—Juvenile literature. 2. Bald eagle—United States—Juvenile literature. 3. Signs
and symbols—United States—Juvenile literature. I. Eldridge, Stephen. II. Title.
  CD5610.E43 2012
  929.9'20973—dc23
                        2011028537
Paperback ISBN 978-1-4644-0047-6
ePUB ISBN 978-1-4645-0954-4
PDF ISBN 978-1-4646-0954-1

Printed in China
012012 Leo Paper Group, Heshan City, Guangdong, China
10 9 8 7 6 5 4 3 2 1

To Our Readers: We have done our best to make sure all Internet Addresses in this book were active and
appropriate when we went to press. However, the author and the publisher have no control over and assume
no liability for the material available on those Internet sites or on other Web sites they may link to. Any
comments or suggestions can be sent by e-mail to comments@enslow.com or to the address on the back
cover.

Photo Credits: All photos by Shutterstock.com, except p 16, © 2011 Photos.com, a division of
Getty Images.

Cover Photo: Shutterstock.com

Note to Parents and Teachers:

Help pre-readers get a jump start on reading. These lively stories introduce simple concepts with repetition
of words and short simple sentences. Photos and illustrations fill the pages with color and effectively
enhance the text. Free Educator Guides are available for this series at www.enslow.com. Search for the *All
About American Symbols* series name.

Contents

Words to Know

free

money

symbol

I see a bald eagle.

The bald eagle is a bird.

It is not really bald!

It has a white head.

The bald eagle is a symbol of America.

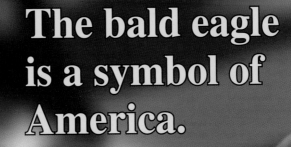

Bald eagles fly high and free.

American people are free.

Where do I see a bald eagle?

I see a bald eagle at the zoo.

I see a bald eagle
in the sky.

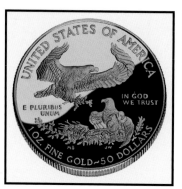 

I see a bald eagle
on money.

I see a bald eagle.

I think of America!

Read More

Arnold, Caroline. *A Bald Eagle's World*. Minneapolis, Minn.: Picture Window Books, 2010.

Stone, Lynn M. *Bald Eagle*. Vero Beach, Fla.: Rourke Pub, 2004.

Worsley, Arlene. *Bald Eagles*. New York: Weigl Publishers, 2007.

Web Sites

National Geographic Kids. *Bald Eagle Facts and Pictures.* © 1996-2010.
<http://kids.nationalgeographic.com/kids/animals/creaturefeature/baldeagle/>

San Diego Zoo. *Bald Eagle*. 2011.
<http://kids.sandiegozoo.org/animals/birds/bald-eagle>

Index

Guided Reading Level: **B**
Guided Reading Leveling System is based on the guidelines recommended by Fountas and Pinnell.

Word Count: 78